HOLIDAYS & HEROES

Let's Celebrate

MARTIN LUTHER KING JR. DAY

BY Barbara deRubertis

ILLUSTRATED BY Gershom Griffith

DR. MARTIN LUTHER KING JR.

The Kane Press • New York

For activities for this book and others in the HOLIDAYS & HEROES series,
visit www.kanepress.com/holidaysandheroes.html.

Library of Congress Cataloging-in-Publication Data

deRubertis, Barbara.
  [Martin Luther King Day]
  Let's celebrate Martin Luther King Jr. Day / by Barbara deRubertis ; illustrated by Gershom Griffith.
    pages cm. -- (Holidays & heroes)
  Original edition published under title: Martin Luther King Day. New York : Kane Press, 1993.
  ISBN 978-1-57565-638-0 (pbk. : alk. paper) -- ISBN 978-1-57565-639-7 (e-book)
  1. Martin Luther King, Jr., Day--Juvenile literature. 2. King, Martin Luther, Jr., 1929-1968--Juvenile
literature. 3. African Americans--Civil rights--History--20th century--Juvenile literature. 4. African
American civil rights workers--Biography--Juvenile literature. 5. Civil rights workers--United States-
-Biography--Juvenile literature. 6. Baptists--United States--Clergy--Biography--Juvenile literature. 7.
African Americans--Biography--Juvenile literature. I. Griffith, Gershom, illustrator. II. Title.
  E185.97.K5D45 2013
  394.261--dc23
                        2013001590

1 3 5 7 9 10 8 6 4 2

Revised edition first published in the United States of America in 2013 by Kane Press, Inc.
Printed in the United States of America

Book Design: Edward Miller
Photograph/Image Research: Maura Taboubi

Visit us online at www.kanepress.com.

 Like us on Facebook
facebook.com/kanepress

 Follow us on Twitter
@kanepress

On the third Monday of January, we celebrate the birthday of an important American, Dr. Martin Luther King Jr.

Dr. King worked hard to change laws and attitudes that were unfair and hurtful to black people.

In his heart he knew that ALL people should be treated with fairness and respect. Fairness was important to Martin Luther King.

Martin Luther King Jr. was born on January 15, 1929, in Atlanta, Georgia. His mother hugged her beautiful baby boy. His father was so happy, he jumped up and touched the ceiling!

Martin's parents were living with his mother's parents in a big house on Auburn Avenue. Martin already had an older sister. The next year, his younger brother was born.

Martin's grandfather was the pastor at Ebenezer Baptist Church. When Martin was two, his grandfather died. Martin's father, Martin Luther King Sr., became the new pastor of the church.

Thirty years later, Martin would also become a pastor at this same church!

Ebenezer Baptist Church, Atlanta, Georgia

Martin's family knew very little about their ancestors—family members who lived a long time ago. But like most black Americans, they knew that many of their ancestors probably had been slaves.

For hundreds of years, African people were brought to America to work as slaves.

Women, men, and children were captured in Africa and taken away from their families and homes.

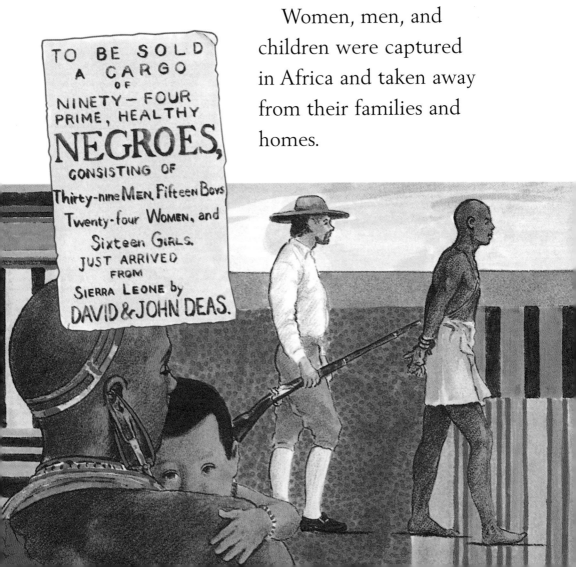

TO BE SOLD
A CARGO
OF
NINETY-FOUR
PRIME, HEALTHY
NEGROES,
CONSISTING OF
Thirty-nine MEN, Fifteen Boys
Twenty-four WOMEN, and
Sixteen GIRLS.
JUST ARRIVED
FROM
SIERRA LEONE by
DAVID & JOHN DEAS.

Sweet potato planting, Hopkinson's Plantation

They were then chained up and put on crowded ships. If they survived the terrible voyage across the ocean, they were sold as slaves when they reached America.

In 1865, slavery finally ended in the United States. But when Martin Luther King was born, there were still many serious problems left over from the time of slavery.

Especially in the South, black people were treated as if they were not as good as white people. Black people were kept separate—or "segregated"—from white people.

In the South, segregation was everywhere.

Neighborhoods. Churches. Schools.
Swimming pools. Libraries. Parks.
Restaurants. Buses. Stores.
Restrooms. Elevators. Water fountains.

The list went on and on. It was very unfair. It was very hurtful. And black people were getting tired of it.

Martin was growing up with people who loved and respected him. He didn't realize at first that there were other people who might feel differently about him.

When Martin was six, he had a white friend whose father owned a store across the street from Martin's house. One day the friend told Martin that they could no longer play together. The friend's father wouldn't allow it.

At dinner that evening, Martin asked his parents why this had happened. Sadly, they explained that it was because Martin's skin was black.

Martin was shocked! It was so unfair. It was so hurtful.

*In his heart he knew that
the color of a person's skin
should not matter to real friends.
Friendship was important
to Martin Luther King.*

A school for black American children, 1942

Martin liked school. He was such a good student, he was allowed to skip two grades.

When he got to college, he found that the work was much harder. But he knew what to do. He just worked harder than ever!

While he was in college, Martin decided he wanted to be a minister like his father. Martin preached his first sermon at Ebenezer Baptist Church. It was a great success!

After graduating from college, Martin went to a seminary, a special school for people who want to become ministers.

There Martin learned that peaceful ways are much more powerful than violence.

Martin decided that he would always try to *love* people—even those who treated him unfairly or hurt his feelings.

Crozer Theological Seminary

When Martin graduated from the seminary, he was the top student in his class. He won a scholarship to attend graduate school at a big university.

After several more years of study, he earned the highest degree a person can receive—a doctorate. Now he was called *Dr.* King!

During this time, Martin met and fell in love with Coretta Scott, a talented young woman who was studying music. After their marriage, Martin was asked to be the pastor of a church in Montgomery, Alabama.

Yolanda, the first of the Kings' four children, was born in 1955. She was followed by Martin III, Dexter, and Bernice. The Kings loved their children, and they wanted them to be treated with kindness and respect.

Martin Luther King with his wife, Coretta, and children Martin III and Yolanda

On December 1, 1955, an important event happened in Montgomery. A black woman named Rosa Parks got on a bus to go home from work. She sat down on a seat in the "colored" section at the back of the bus. Soon all the seats in both the "colored" section and the "white" section were full.

Then a white man boarded the bus. The driver told Mrs. Parks that she had to give up her seat. When she refused, she was arrested.

Rosa Parks

Martin Luther King speaks about the bus boycott to an overflow crowd at the Holt Street Baptist Church in Montgomery, Alabama.

The black people of Montgomery decided to protest. They refused to ride the buses until the unfair rules changed. This was called a "boycott," and Dr. King became its leader.

The Montgomery bus boycott lasted 382 days—more than a year! When it was over, black people could sit wherever they liked on a bus. And they no longer had to give up their seats to white people. They had won an important victory, and they had won it peacefully.

Martin Luther King delivers a sermon in Atlanta, Georgia.

In 1960, Dr. King was asked to come back to Atlanta, Georgia. He became co-pastor with his father at Ebenezer Baptist Church.

Also, Dr. King was the president of an important new "civil rights" group. This group wanted black people to have the same rights that white Americans had.

In his heart he knew
that Americans of all colors
should have the same rights.
Equal rights were important
to Martin Luther King.

At this time, more and more white people were joining black people in the work for equal rights.

Black and white students together held "sit-ins" at lunch counters for "whites only." They simply sat down and waited to be served. Day after day, the students returned to sit and wait. Sometimes they also sang songs like "We Shall Overcome."

When Dr. King joined a sit-in at a lunch counter in Atlanta, he was arrested and put in jail for several days.

A sit-in in Nashville, Tennessee

Martin Luther King leads a line of marchers toward Birmingham, Alabama.

In the spring of 1963, Dr. King went to Birmingham, Alabama, one of the most segregated cities in the South. Dr. King helped black people there plan protest marches. He always reminded the marchers not to use any kind of violence.

Thousands of children and young people joined the peaceful marches. But one day, police suddenly turned fire hoses and attack dogs onto the marchers!

People across America were horrified!

Two days later, another march began. This time, police refused to follow orders to attack the marchers.

Soon afterward, life began to get better for black people in Birmingham—thanks to the courage of Dr. King and those who marched with him.

In his heart he knew
that peaceful protest is more powerful
than violence.
Nonviolence was important
to Martin Luther King.

Statue of Dr. Martin Luther King Jr. in Birmingham, Alabama

During the summer of 1963, Dr. King
organized the March on Washington.
More than 250,000 people—black and white,
rich and poor—came to our nation's capital.

On August 28, they all marched to the
Lincoln Memorial. There they heard
many speeches about the importance of
equal rights for ALL Americans.

The one speech that everyone still
remembers was given by Dr. King.

"I have a dream that one day . . . little black boys and black girls will be able to join hands with little white boys and white girls as sisters and brothers. I have a dream today!"

*In his heart he knew
that his dream of a better America
would come true—someday.
Dreams were important
to Martin Luther King.*

March on Washington. Demonstrators fill the lawn in front of the Lincoln Memorial.

In 1964, an important civil rights act was signed by the President of the United States. Segregation was now against the law!

Neighborhoods. Churches. Schools.
Swimming pools. Libraries. Parks.
Restaurants. Buses. Stores.
Restrooms. Elevators. Water fountains.

At last, black people were free to go anywhere they chose.

Martin Luther King is congratulated after receiving the Nobel Peace Prize in Oslo, Norway.

Later in 1964, Dr. King was given the Nobel Peace Prize, the greatest of his many honors. This award is given to those who have done the most to bring peace to the world.

Dr. King said that the award really belonged to the thousands of people who had worked with him. He gave the prize money— $54,000—to groups working for civil rights.

Martin Luther King speaks to the crowd in Montgomery, Alabama, after a five-day civil rights march from Selma.

In 1965, Dr. King went to Selma, Alabama, to help black people register to vote. Some white people there did not want black people to vote in elections. Trouble soon began.

Dr. King called for a protest march from Selma to Montgomery, the state capital. Again, police attacked the marchers.

Again, people across America were very upset when they heard the news. Hundreds of people—both black and white—rushed to Selma to join the march.

The President of the United States sent 1,800 soldiers to protect the marchers.

When the marchers finally arrived in Montgomery, they had walked over 50 miles in five days. And they had won the support of millions of Americans.

The President now began to work for a law that would make it easier for black people to register and vote.

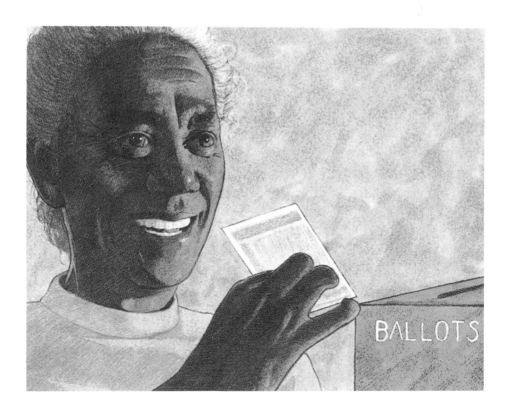

On April 3, 1968, Dr. King went to Memphis, Tennessee. Black sanitation workers there had asked him to help with a march for fair pay.

The night after he arrived, Dr. King gave a speech. He said that he knew life would soon get better for black people in America.

"I've been to the mountaintop. . . .
And I've seen the promised land.
I may not get there with you.
But I want you to know tonight, that we, as a people, will get to the promised land."

The next day, Dr. King was shot and killed.

A wreath for Martin Luther King Jr. in Memphis, Tennessee

Dr. King was only thirty-nine years old when he died.

During his short life, he had worked hard. Thousands of other people, of all colors, had worked with him. Together, they had been able to change some of the laws and attitudes that were unfair and hurtful to black people.

Demonstrators in front of the White House after the death of Martin Luther King

But the work was not finished. It would be up to others to carry on the work of Dr. King. It would be up to others to make peace.

In his heart he knew
that people of all colors
can live together in peace and harmony.
Peace was important
to Martin Luther King.

When we celebrate the birthday of Dr. Martin Luther King Jr., we remember his dream. How can we keep the dream alive?

In our hearts we know
that we can treat ALL people
with fairness and respect.
We can carry on the work
of Martin Luther King.